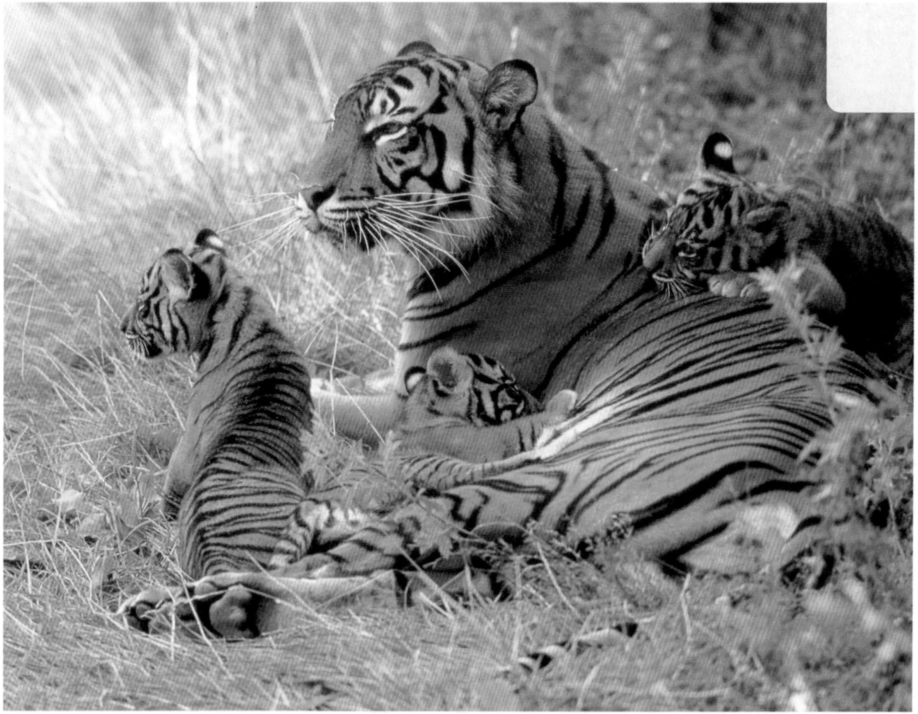

We saw the tigers.

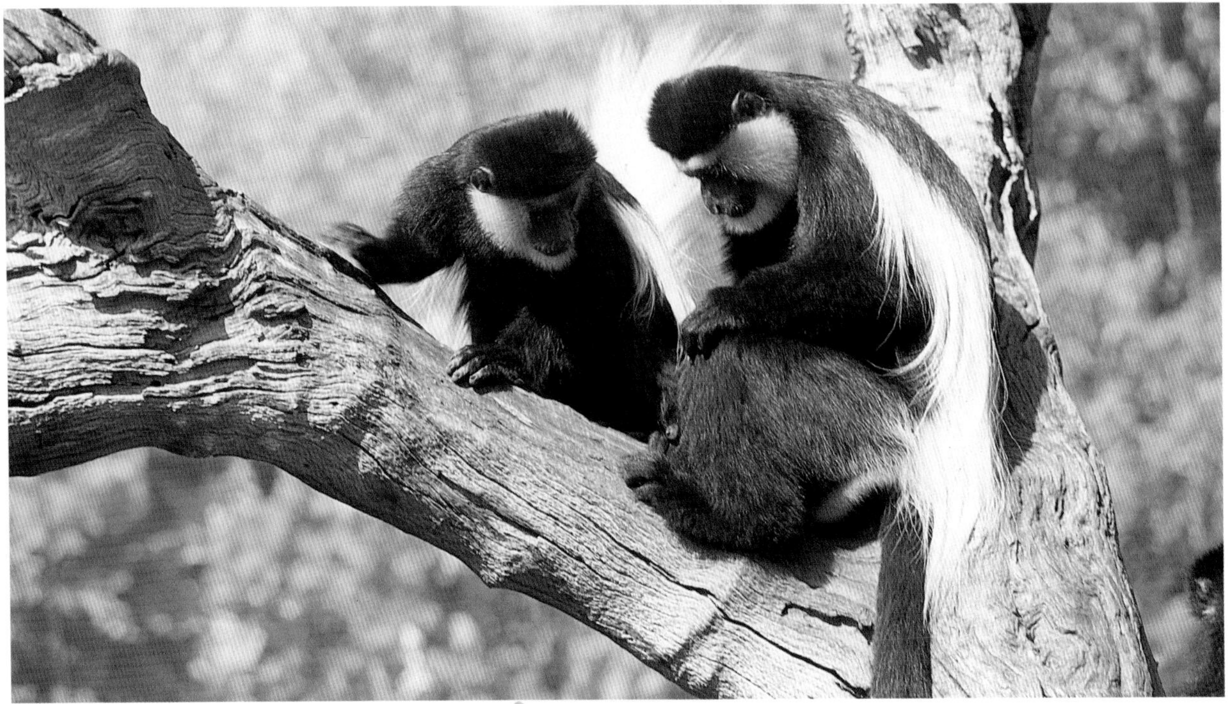

We saw the monkeys.

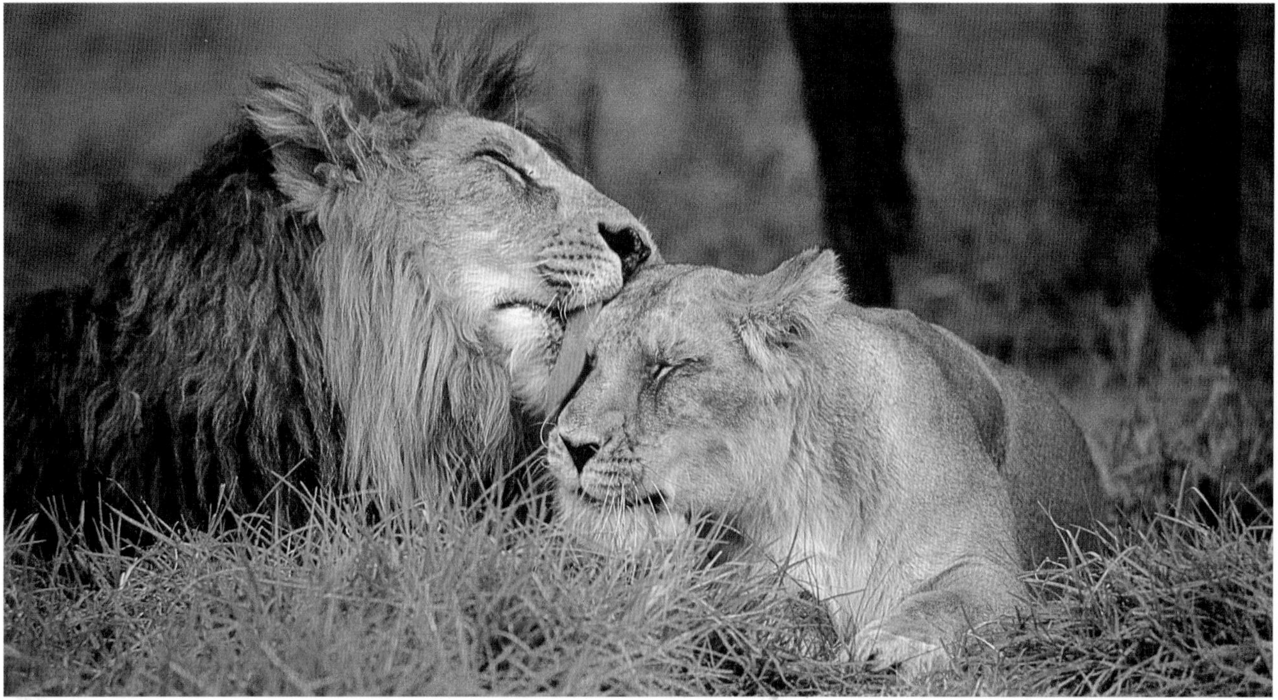

We saw the lions.

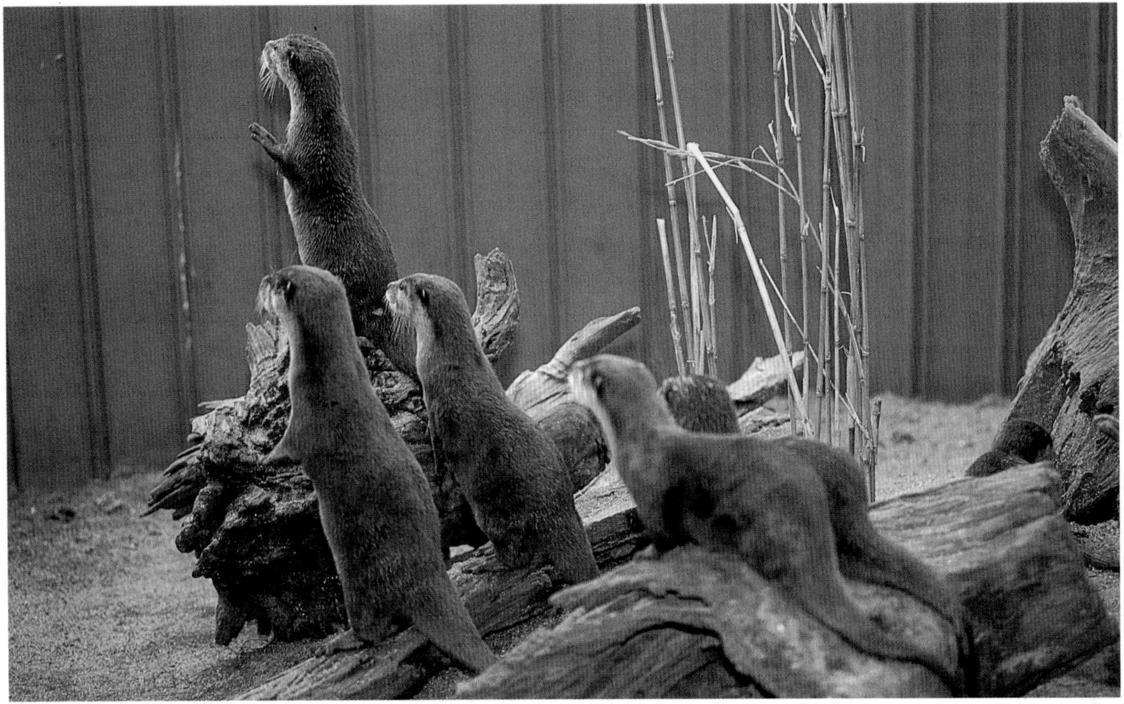

We saw the otters.

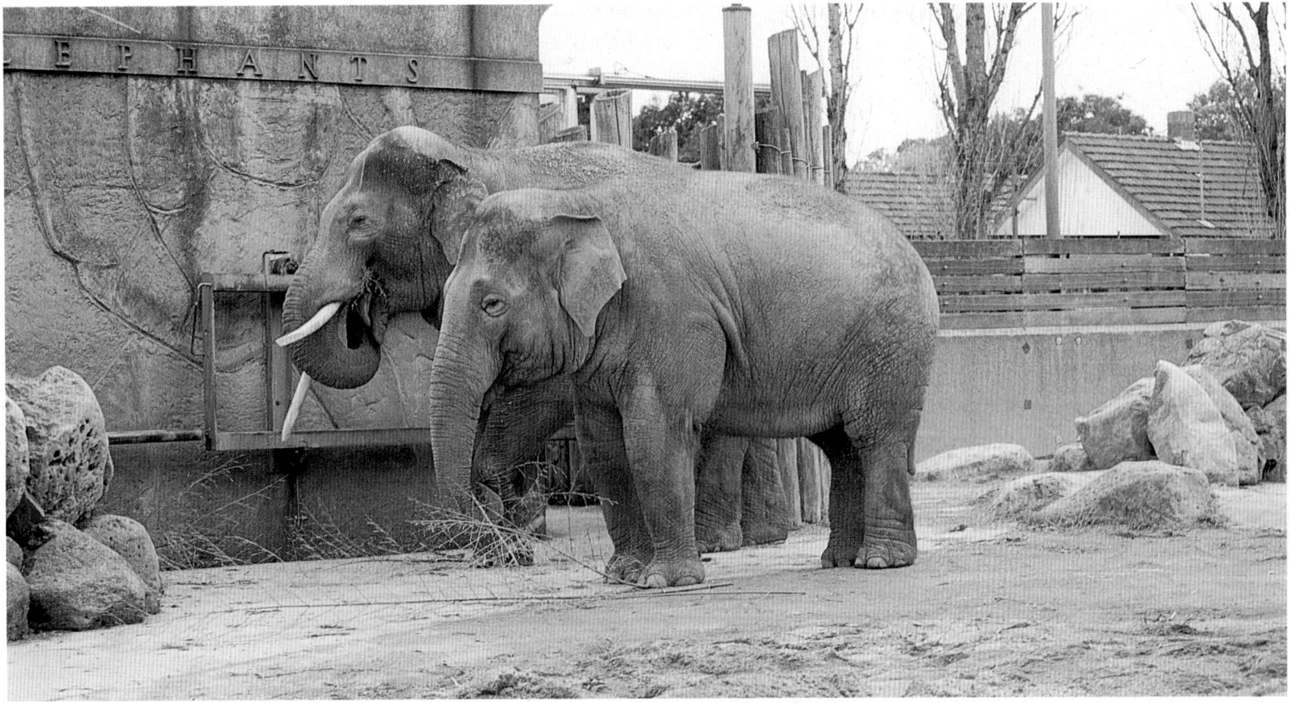

We saw the elephants.

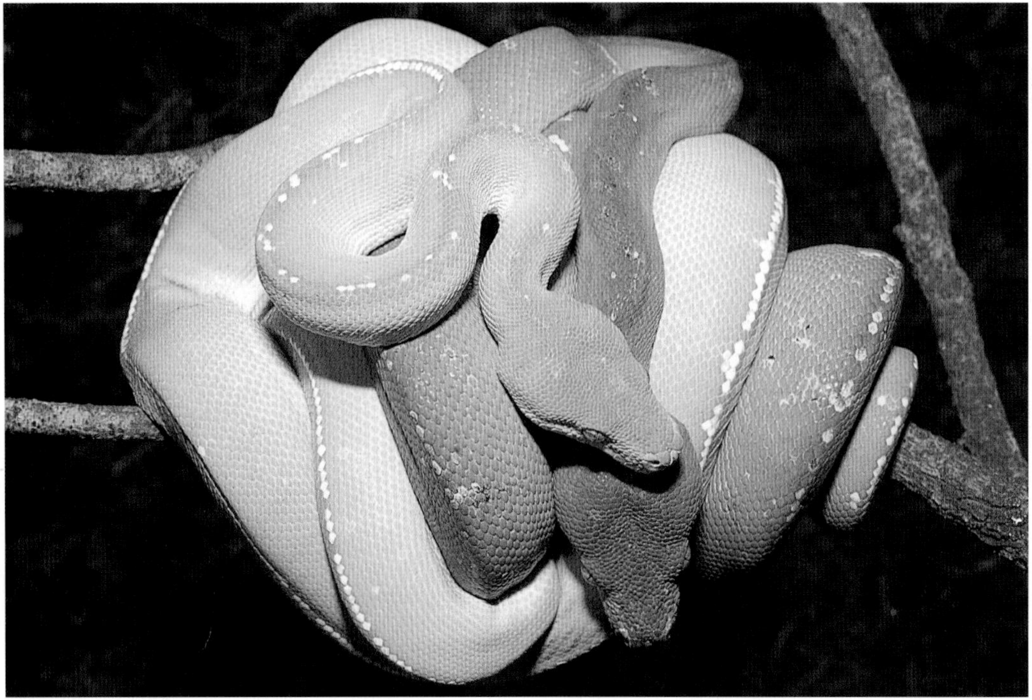

We saw the snakes.

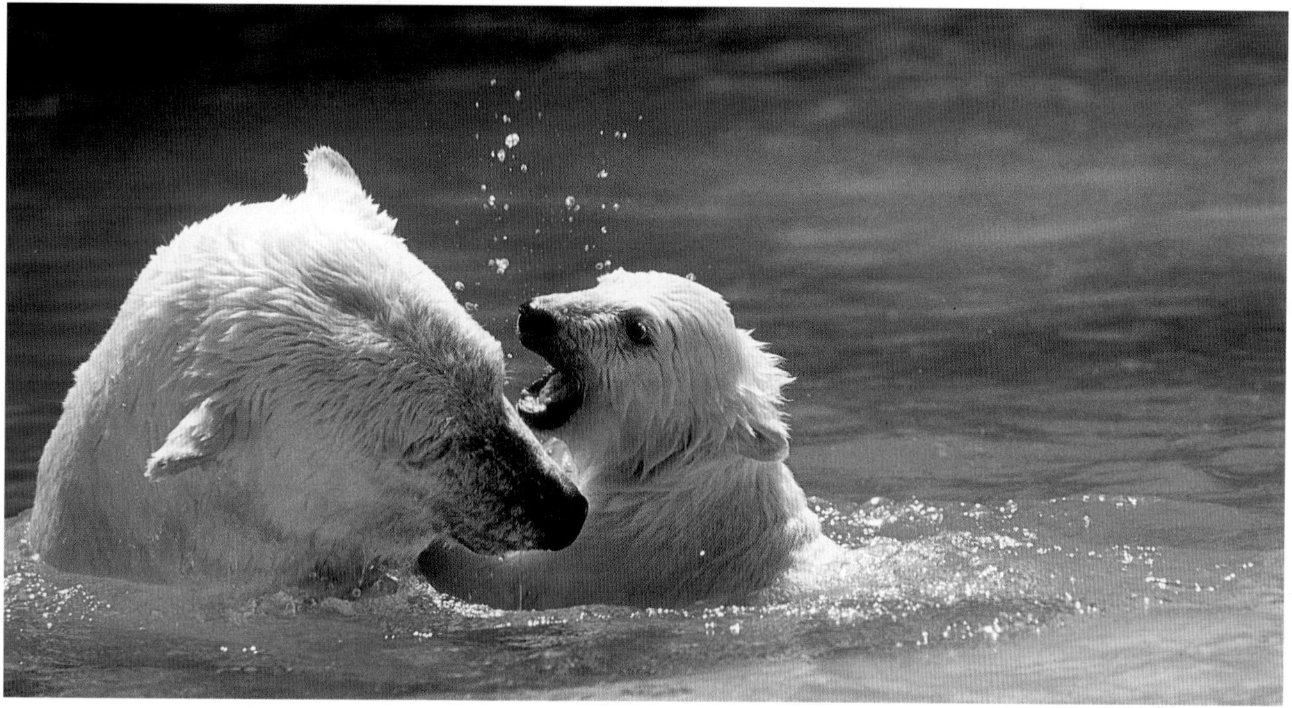

We saw the bears.

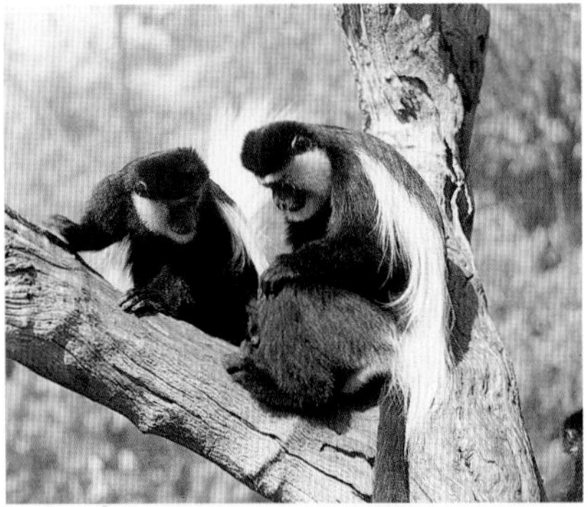
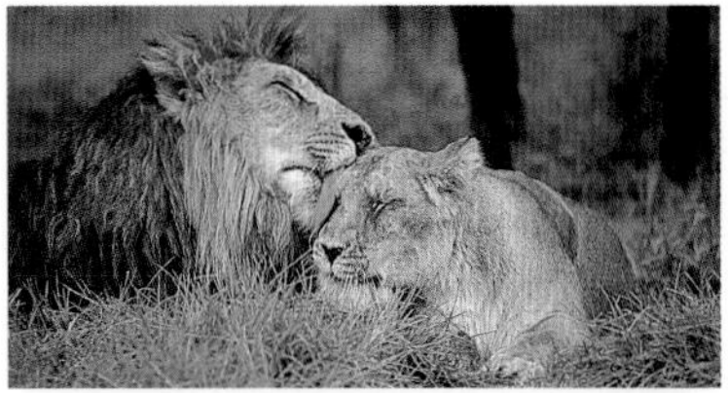
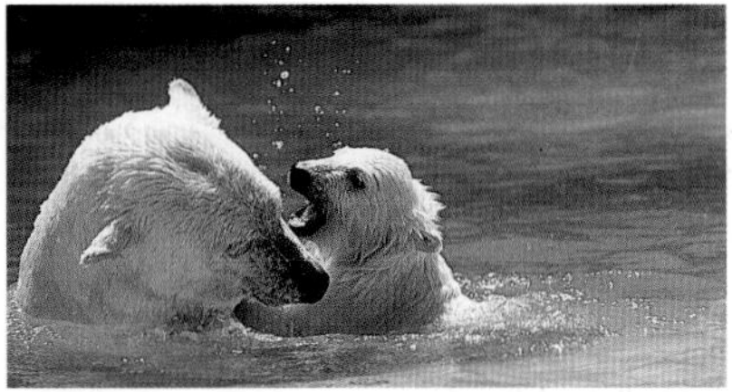
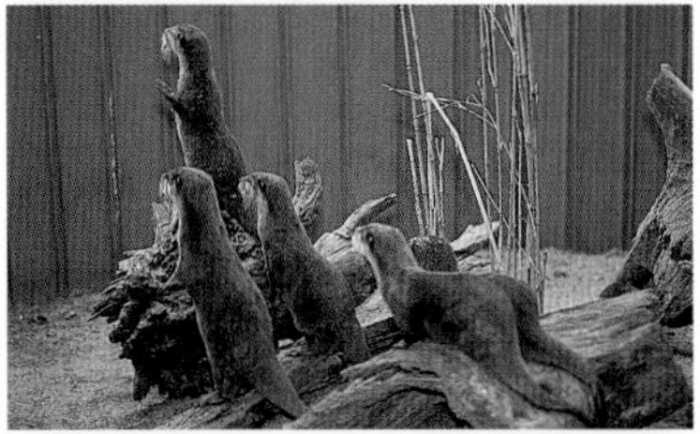
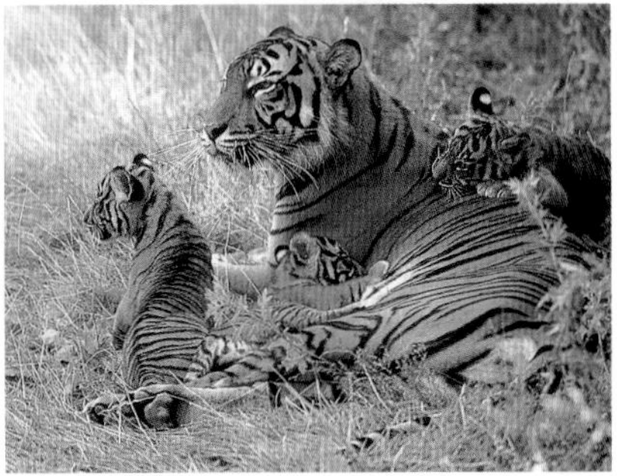
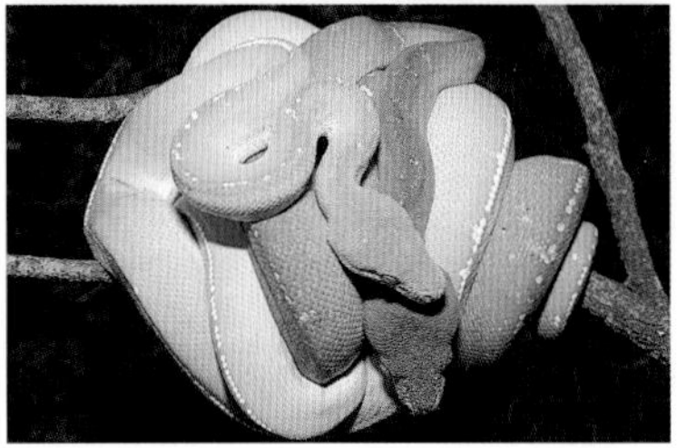
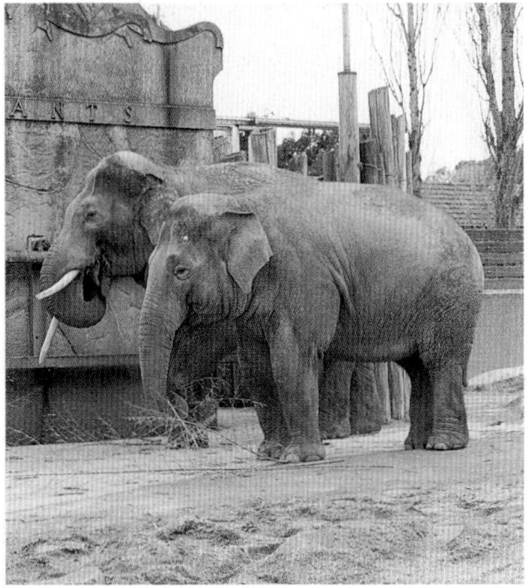

We saw many animals.